For: Crispin
From: A.T.B.

To the 'girls' -
Tamsy, Amy and Becky
D.P.

First published in the UK 2005 by Mathew Price Ltd,
The Old Glove Factory, Bristol Road,
Sherborne, Dorset DT9 4HP

Designed by Matthew Lilly

Manufactured in China

ISBN 1-84248-165-7

Magnificent Mazes
Dinosaur Trails

Anna
Nilsen

How to Play
Find out through
the time tunnel.

TIME TUNNEL

Written by
Douglas Palmer

Mathew Price Limited

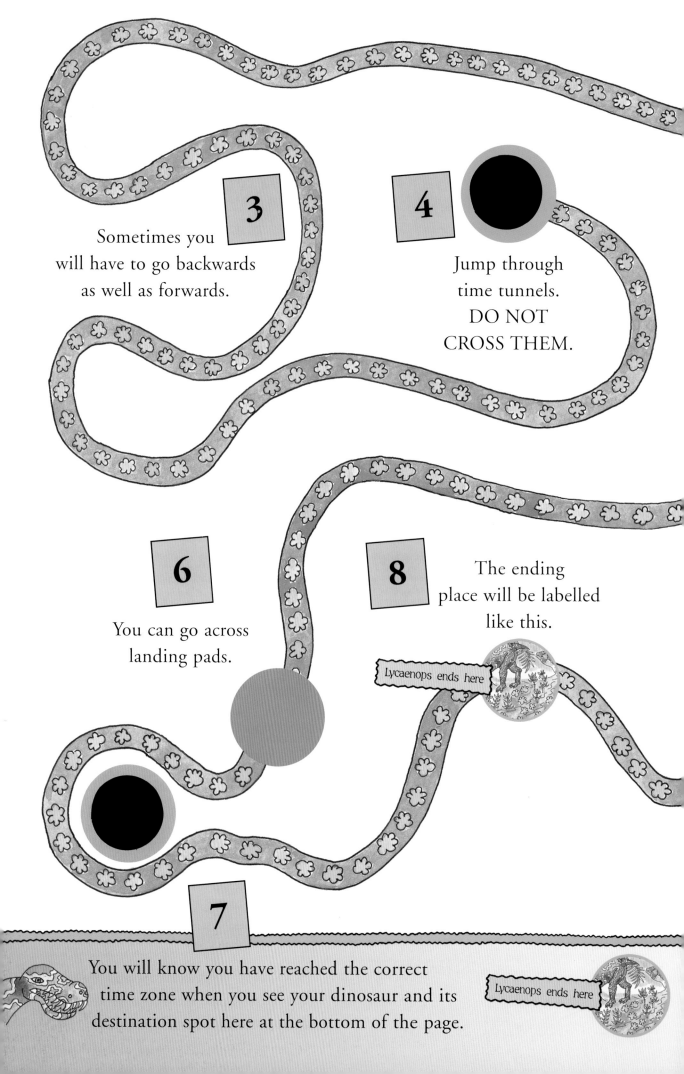

3

Sometimes you will have to go backwards as well as forwards.

4

Jump through time tunnels.
DO NOT
CROSS THEM.

6

You can go across landing pads.

8

The ending place will be labelled like this.

Lycaenops ends here

7

You will know you have reached the correct time zone when you see your dinosaur and its destination spot here at the bottom of the page.

Lycaenops ends here

5

When you jump through a time tunnel you will arrive on a landing pad. Choose a path and carry on.

10

Choose another dinosaur or go to the back of the book for more fun.

Lycaenops starts here

2

Lead your chosen dinosaur through the maze...

1

Lycaenops

Choose a dinosaur from a tab and find it in the picture.

LANDING PAD

How to Play

Follow the numbers 1 to 10 and learn how to play the game.

9

Each time zone has three extra details for you to find. They will appear here.

Acanthostega

365 million years ago the first primitive plants
to live on land grew by hot swampy rivers and lakes.

Acanthostega
ends here

Archaeopteryx starts here

Acanthostega ends here

These waters teemed with strange armoured fish and the first four-legged animals, such as Acanthostega.

Can you find these three details?

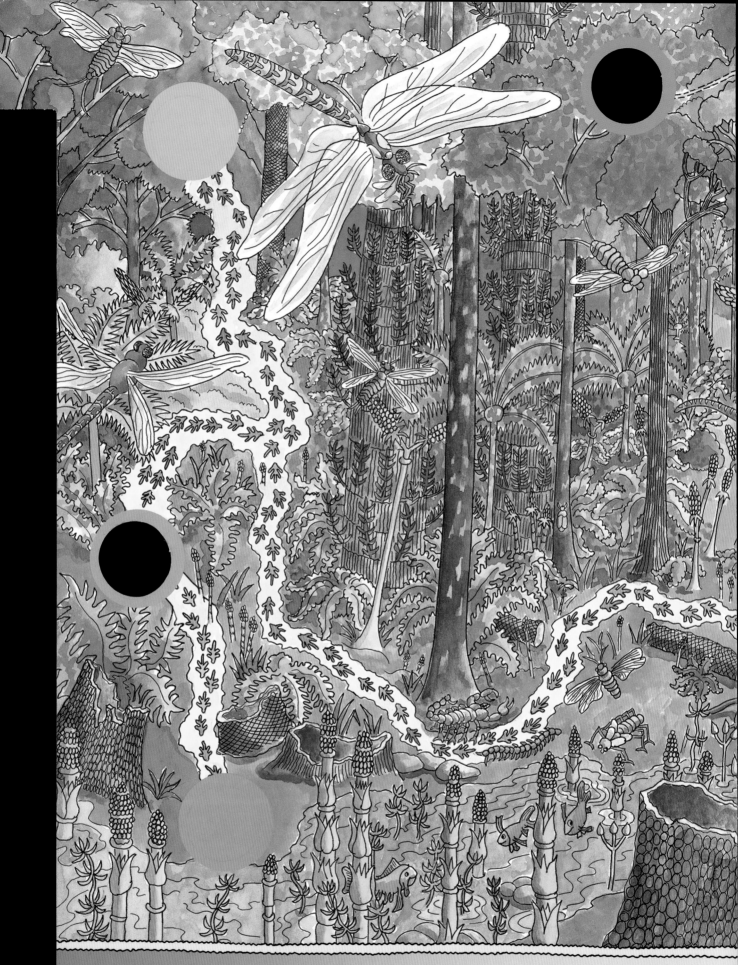

Hylonomus

310 million years ago the vast tropical rain forests
and swamps formed the first coal deposits on Earth.

Hylonomus
ends here

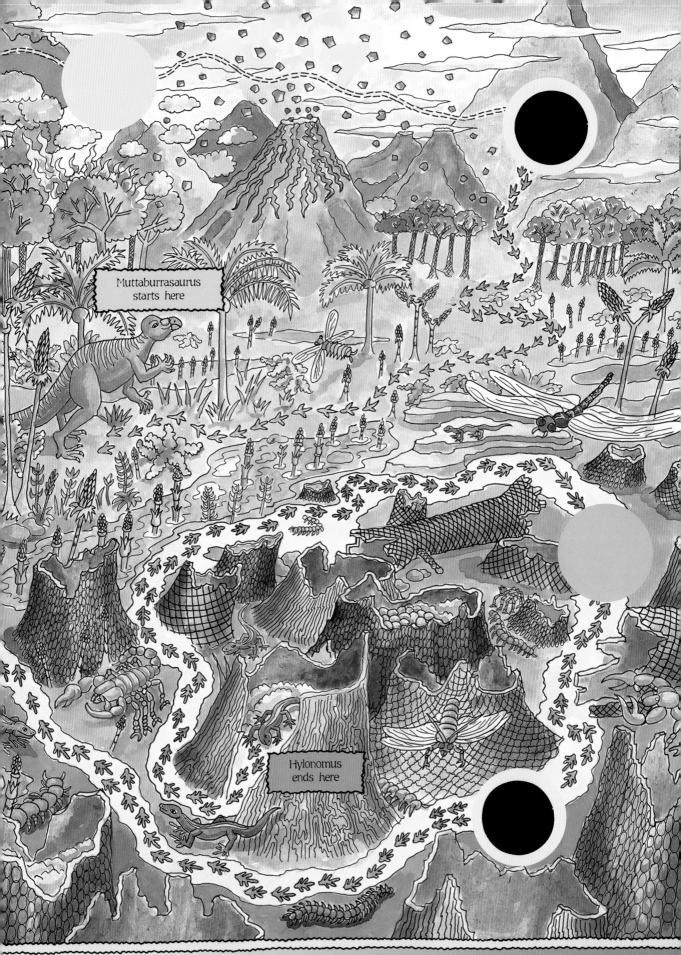

Muttaburrasaurus
starts here

Hylonomus
ends here

These forests in Canada were home to many
creatures from giant dragonflies to the first reptiles,
such as Hylonomus.

Can you find these three details?

Lycaenops

Southern Africa 255 million years ago had
some of the first predators on earth.

Lycaenops ends here

Rhamphorhynchus starts here

Lycaenops ends here

There was Lycaenops, which hunted plant-eating
reptiles like Dicynodon or Milleretta, and
Peltrobatrachus, which ate fish and small animals.

Can you find these three details?

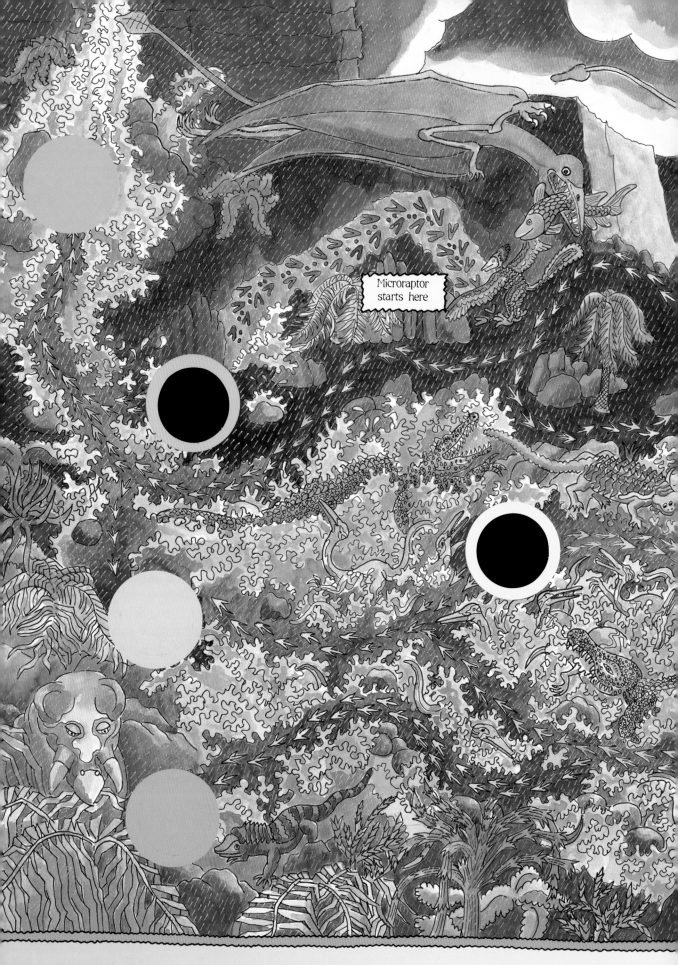

Microraptor
starts here

Coelophysis

215 million years ago, a herd of a thousand small
dinosaurs - and other creatures that lived nearby –

Coelophysis
ends here

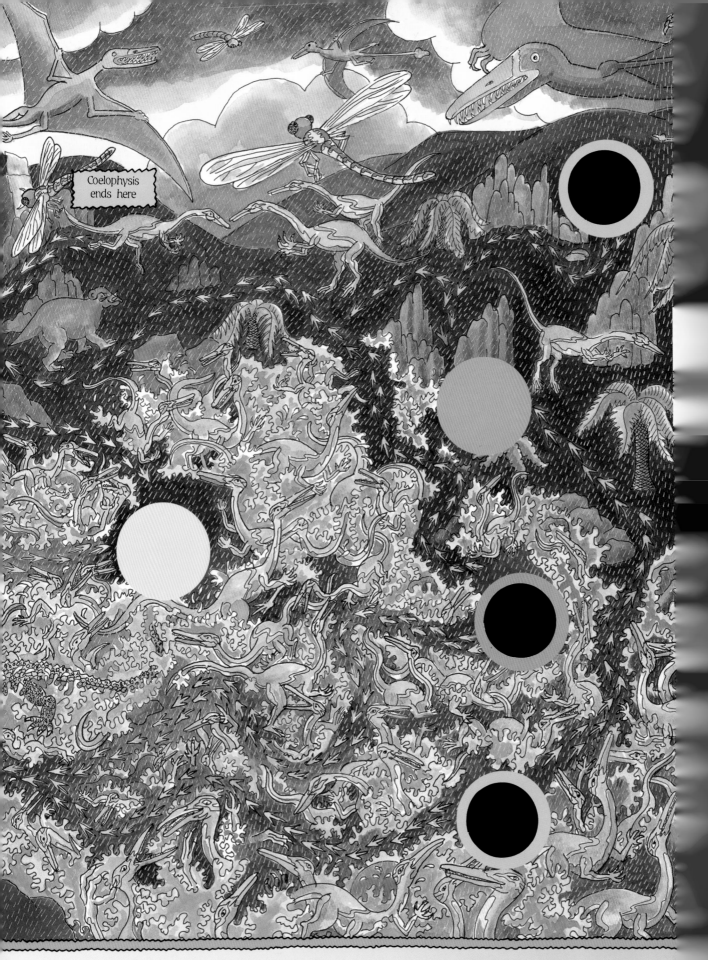

Coelophysis
ends here

were overwhelmed by a sudden flood of river water.
Their fossilized remains were discovered in New
Mexico, USA, in 1947.

Can you find these three details?

Rhamphorhynchus ends here

Rhamphorhynchus

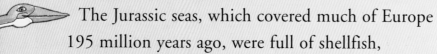

The Jurassic seas, which covered much of Europe 195 million years ago, were full of shellfish,

Rhamphorhynchus ends here

Hylonomus
starts here

ammonites and fish. The fish were eaten by reptiles,
such as ichthyosaurs, long necked plesiosaurs and
flying pterosaurs like Rhamphorhynchus.

Can you find these three details?

Archaeopteryx
ends here

Archaeopteryx

By Jurassic times there were many different
kinds of dinosaurs of all shapes and sizes.

Archaeopteryx
ends here

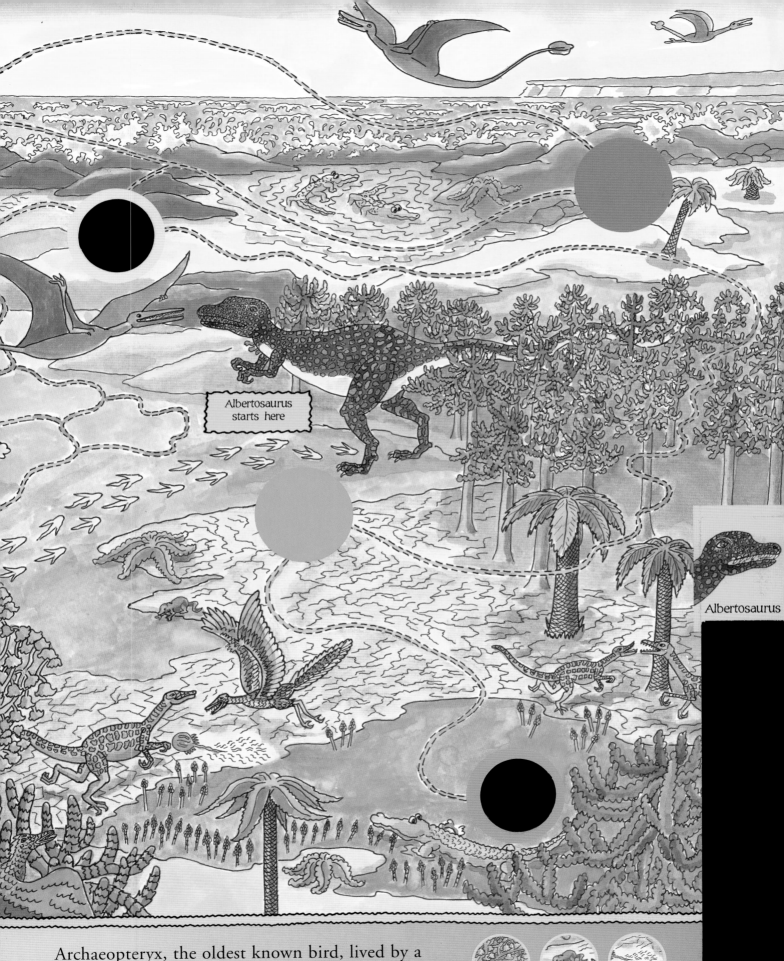

Albertosaurus
starts here

Albertosaurus

Archaeopteryx, the oldest known bird, lived by a
lagoon in what is now Germany, alongside some small
two-legged dinosaurs, called Compsognathus.

Can you find these three details?

Coelophysis
starts here

Muttaburrasaurus

Muttaburrasaurus lived 130 million years ago,
eating plants in the cold forests of Cretaceous Australia.

Muttaburrasaurus
ends here

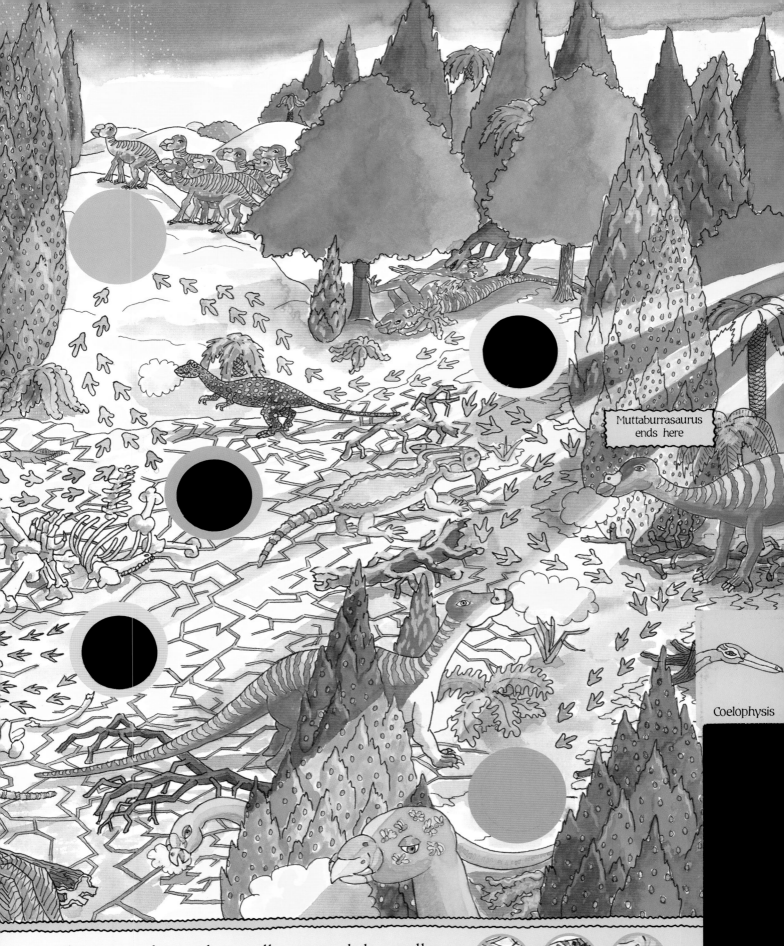

Muttaburrasaurus ends here

Coelophysis

There were also predatory allosaurs and the smaller Leaellynasaura. A huge, 5m long amphibian called Koolasuchus moved between water and land.

Can you find these three details?

Microraptor
ends here

Microraptor

Many amazing fossils have been found in the
ancient sediments from lakes in China.

Microraptor
ends here

Lycaenops
starts here

Lycaenops

They include small, feathered dinosaurs from the
Cretaceous age, such as the four-winged, gliding
Microraptor, and other closely related birds.

Can you find these three details?

Propalaeotherium
starts here

Albertosaurus
ends here

Albertosaurus

Cretaceous times were brought to an end by a catastrophe: an asteroid collided with the Earth.

Albertosaurus
ends here

All the dinosaurs died except for the feathered ones
we know as birds. Reptiles, such as the crocodiles
survived, and small, hairy mammals - our ancestors.

Propalaeotheriu

Can you find these three details?

Propalaeotherium

50 million years ago all non-feathered dinosaurs had died out. Birds, mammals and the remaining reptiles –

Propalaeotherium
ends here

Propalaeotherium ends here

Acanthostega starts here

crocodiles, lizards and snakes – all began to flourish.
Fossils from a subtropical wooded lake in Germany
open a window onto life in Eocene times.

Can you find these three details?

Acanthostega

Continents on the Move

The lands and seas of the world look like this today but they have not always been so arranged. The continents have moved around as oceans have opened and closed.

365 million years ago the world looked very different. Acanthostega lived in Greenland, part of a huge land mass stretching from North America to Europe.

In Carboniferous times 310 million years ago Hylonomus lived in Nova Scotia within tropical coal forests which spread from America to Russia.

By 255 million years ago almost all the continents were joined together to form one huge landmass called Pangea. Lycaenops lived in the cool climate of Southern Africa.

Much of the Pangean landmass was desert in Triassic times but early dinosaurs such as Coelophysis, thrived in New Mexico where there was plenty of small animals to eat.

A long time ago

Acanthostega
365m years ago

Hylonomus
310m years ago

Lycaenops
255m years ago

Coelophysis
215m years ago

Rhamphorhynchus
195m years ago

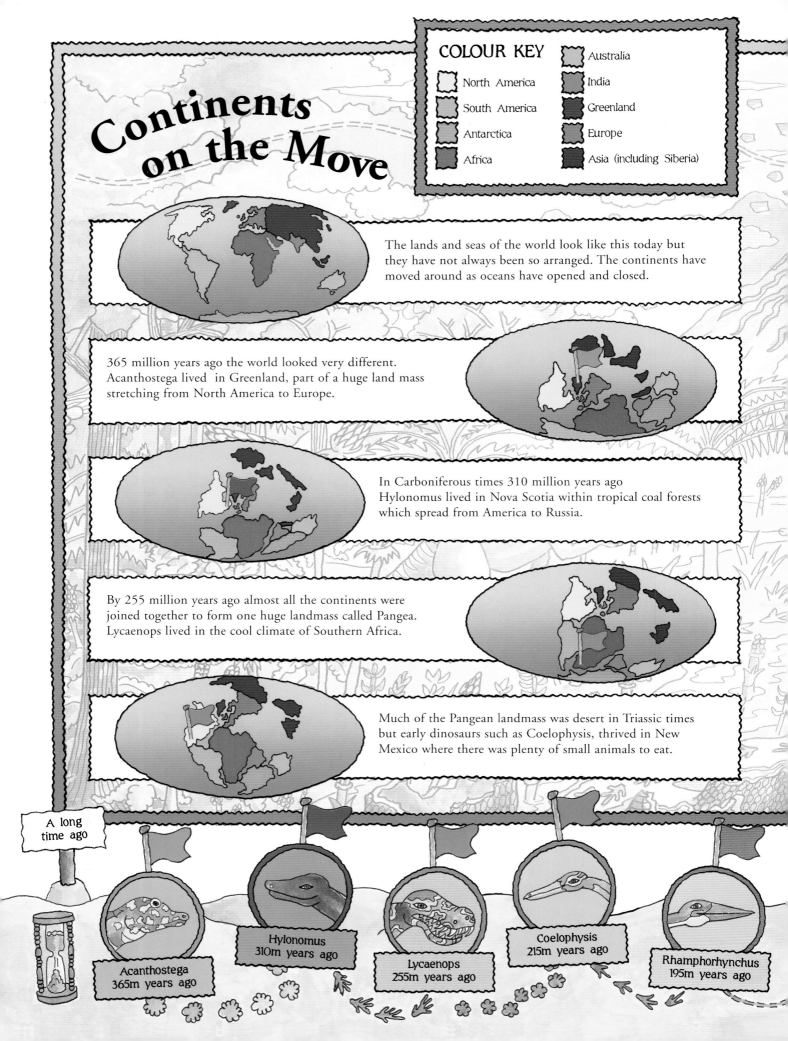

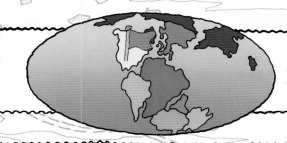

By 195 million years ago Pangea broke apart and flying reptiles such as Rhamphorhynchus soared from cliffs over seas crowded with fish and swimming reptiles such as the ichthyosaurs.

By 155 million years ago North America had broken away from Africa forming a new seaway which we call the Atlantic Ocean and Archaeopteryx lived by the sea in southern Germany.

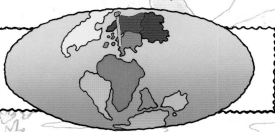

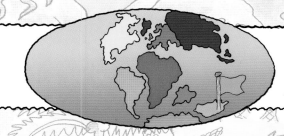

By 130 million years ago, a huge seaway separated the northern continents from those in the south. Muttaburrasaurus lived in Australia which had cold climate and dark winters in Cretaceous times.

As the South Atlantic was growing bigger 124 million years ago, there were lots of different kinds of feathered dinosaurs like Microraptor from China.

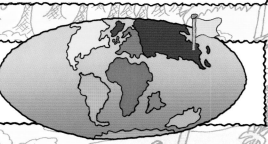

65 million years ago a huge asteroid from space crashed into the Earth causing giant waves, forest fires and climate change that killed off many plants and animals including the dinosaurs.

By Eocene times, 50 million years ago, the world looks much more familiar. The one continent that was still very much on the move was India. The Himalayan mountains were formed when India crashed into Asia.

Archaeopteryx
155m years ago

Muttaburrasaurus
130m years ago

Microraptor
124m years ago

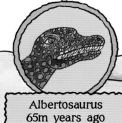

Albertosaurus
65m years ago

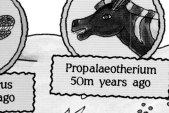

Propalaeotherium
50m years ago

Quite recently

Telescope Game

How much did you really notice along the maze routes? Look at these views and see if you know where they came from.

Muttaburrasaurus had a hollow nose bump which may have amplified its call sounds.

Sea dwelling sealilies are plant-like animals, here rooted to a floating log.

Microraptor was an amazing four-winged dinosaur which could glide from tree to tree.

Bony ribs stiffened the wings of gliding lizards such as Coelurosauravus.

Crocodiles predated the dinosaurs and are the most ancient surviving reptile groups.

The flattened end to Eudimorphodon's tail helped balance and steer the animal's flight.

Eudimorphodon's hand has three claw-like fingers and a long fourth which supports the wing.

Pteraspis was one of the strange bony plated but jawless fish that lived in Devonian rivers.

Compsognathus was a small two-legged dinosaur like Archaeopteryx but without feathers.

Some of the first leaf-cutting ants have been found fossilised at Messel.

The lakebed sediments preserve a lot of aquatic plants, such as water lilies.

The coelacanths are a very ancient group of fish which still survive today.

Living horsetails are small but in some ancient forests they grow to 10m high.

With two pairs of strong fins lungfish can crawl out of one pond into another.

Giant centipedes lived amongst the rotting leaves on the forest floor.

The living fossil Ginkgo or maiden-hair tree has survived since Jurassic times.

Flowering plants such as Magnolia had appeared by Cretaceous times.

The first land plants like this Sciadophyton had pale green stems but no leaves.

With its wingspan of 12m Quetzalcoatlus was one of the biggest animals to fly.

Many dinosaurs like crocodiles and birds made nests in which to lay their eggs.

Procynosuchus was a landliving reptile which had otter-like limbs for swimming.

Europolemur was a small lemur-like primate which lived in the trees.

Truly modern birds such as Confuciusornis lived alongside feathered dinosaurs.

Although a bird, Archaeopteryx had a reptile-like long, bony tail, covered in feathers.

Landliving and predatory scorpions such as Pulmonoscorpius grew to 70cm long.

Turtles were one group of reptiles which survived the end of Cretaceous extinction.

Acanthostega had a solid bony skull and jaws.

The crocodile-like Rutiodon grew to 3m long and would attack any potential prey animal.

Sharks have been common fish eating predators since Carboniferous times.

The bullet shaped belemnites were like the 'bones' of living cuttlefish.

Dino Log

What were they and when did they live?

Acanthostega

One of the first four-legged animals on Earth, it lived some 365 million years ago. It grew to around 1m long and looked like a giant newt or salamander, with a long fish-like tail. Acanthostega's legs were used mainly for swimming in rivers and lakes. But it may also have used its front legs to dig up small prey creatures hiding in the riverbed sands and mud. Its descendants used their legs to leave the water and walk on dry land for the first time. Acanthostega is one of the ancestors of dinosaurs and one of our ancestors too.

Hylonomus

Hylonomus had a long tail like a lizard and was one of the first animals to lay eggs, so it was a reptile. Laying eggs with a protective shell surrounding the baby inside allowed Hylonomus to live and reproduce on dry land. It is likely that it could also swim when it needed to. Hylonomus lived in the hot, steamy swamps and forests of Carboniferous times around 310 million years ago. It was quite small, growing to 20 cm long and had a mouth full of lots of small sharp teeth. They were used for crunching its favourite food – the grubs and insects living in the plants which grew all around.

Lycaenops

The name Lycaenops means 'wolf-face.' It was given to this fossil animal because of its long, dagger-like canine teeth. Although only 1 m long, it was one of the first meat-eating land predators and may have hunted in packs. Lycaenops had long legs and could run faster than most other animals of the time. The prey was killed by stabbing bites to its neck and throat. Lycaenops lived in southern Africa during Permian times around 255 million years ago. It was from reptiles like this that the first mammals evolved.

Coelophysis

Coelophysis was one of the earliest true dinosaurs. Growing to 2 m long, it was a fast running and ferocious hunter. It lived in North America in Triassic times around 215 million years ago. The fossil remains of masses of Coelophysis of different ages have been found jumbled together in one place. From this, it seems that they lived in large flocks and sometimes died together, probably overwhelmed by a sudden flood. There is also evidence that they were cannibals and ate just about anything that moved. The fossils of adults have been found with the remains of Coelophysis babies in their stomachs.

Rhamphorhynchus

Rhamphorhynchus was a pterosaur - a flying reptile, one of many different kinds which lived amongst the dinosaurs in Jurassic times. The wings are made of a skin membrane stretched between the arm and finger bones. With a wing span of up to 1.8 m, it was small compared with some pterosaurs, which had wing spans of up to 12m. It fed on fish, which it caught as it skimmed over the waves. Its beak-like jaws were full of long, sharp, interlocking teeth, good for holding slippery fish. Like seabirds today they lived in colonies, where they were safe from predators.

Archaeopteryx

Archaeopteryx was one of the first birds and lived in Europe during late Jurassic times around 155 million years ago. It was about the size of a pigeon and could certainly fly but perhaps not very fast. It flew from tree to tree to escape from predators and gather food. Archaeopteryx was actually a mixture of bird and reptile. It was descended from small carnivorous, feathered dinosaurs and had a long bony tail, clawed hands and a beak armed with lots of sharp teeth. In the mid 19th century, the discovery of the first Archaeopteryx fossil provided strong support for Darwin's theory of evolution.

Muttaburrasaurus

Muttaburrasaurus was a large 10 m long, plant eating dinosaur which lived in Australia during early Cretaceous times 130 million years ago. At that time Australia was near the South Pole and the climate was cold and dark in the winter. Muttaburrasaurus had a massive muscular tail and powerful hind legs which were much bigger than the front legs. Normally it walked on all fours but could rise up on its hind legs and grasp trees with its large thumb spike to reach high leaves. The large bony lump on its nose may have been to do with its well developed sense of smell and for sexual display.

Microraptor

Microraptor was an amazing chicken-sized dinosaur that lived in Cretaceous times 124 million years ago. Microraptor probably spent its life in the trees, using hand claws on its wings to climb after insects and small animals. It had wing-like feathers on both its arms and legs; from high up it could glide from tree to tree in search for food and to escape its enemies. Microraptor is just one of many fantastic fossils found recently in China, which show how birds evolved from feathered dinosaurs like this.

Albertosaurus

Albertosaurus was a huge tyrannosaur with strong hind legs and a heavy muscular tail. It lived in North America at the end of Cretaceous times, 70 million years ago. It wasn't the biggest tyrannosaur but it grew to some 12 m long and could probably run on its hind legs as fast as 25 miles an hour. Although its arms were tiny and had only two claws, its skull was huge. The muscular jaws were armed with an impressive array of curved and blade-shaped serrated teeth, as sharp as steak knives. It had an incredibly powerful bite and could kill large animals.

Propalaeotherium

Propalaeotherium was a little dog-sized, primitive horse. It grew to just 60 cm high at the shoulder. Being so small, it could live and move around in dense forests, safe from large predators. It fed by browsing on the tender leaves of undergrowth shrubs. It had four toes on its front feet and three on the back ones and each toe ended in a tiny hoof. By Eocene times around 50 million years ago, when Propalaeotherium lived, all the dinosaurs had died out. Lots of new kinds of mammals were evolving to replace them including many different kinds of horses which became bigger as they moved out of the forests into open grasslands.